Squishy Wishy Meatballs

By Amelia Griggs

Illustrated by Winda Mulyasari

Dedication

To my Mother, who taught me the joys of cooking.

To my Children, who I love more than life itself.

To my loving Husband, for your never-ending love and support.

It's early Sunday morning.
And Mama's in the kitchen.
What's she doing now?
She's stirring and she's mixin'!

"I wanna help, I wanna help!"
I leaped up and down.

I giggled and I hiccupped.
And I danced all around!

"Are we having pasta?"
"And meatballs too?"
"I can't wait to help."
"Tell me what to do!"

Mama started smiling.
And handed me a spoon.
"It's for our Sunday dinner."
"Not 'til the afternoon!"

"Yes, I know! Yes, I know!"
"But I'm hungry now!"
I spied somethin' in a bowl.
It made my belly growl!

I have to eat my cereal.
And then she'll let me help.

So real quick, I ate it up.
And screamed a big loud "Yelp!"

"I'm ready now! I'm ready now!" I ran over to see.
What is Mama mixin'? What on earth could it be?

Mama's mixin' up the meatballs.
She shapes them in her hand.

She fries them in some oil.
In a great big round hot pan.

She puts them in a pot with sauce.
So they can simmer and cook.

She lifts me up, high in the sky!
So I can take a look!

Mama swung me, 'round her waist.
I laughed a big fat cry!
She said, "We're havin' so much fun."
"But I have to finish 'n fry!"

"I wanna make a meatball!"
"It would be so much fun!"
"Please Mama, please!"
"Can I try and make just one?"

Mama nodded, yes you can!
She pointed to the sink.
"First you have to
wash your hands!"
I did that in a blink!

I rolled a scoop of meat
around in a little ball.
It was very weird and squishy.
But I liked it after all!

So I made a few more meatballs.
And Mama fried some more!
They were squishy wishy meatballs!
But it was a FUN kind of chore!

"Watch and learn and you shall see!"
Said Mama, with a smile.
"Some elbow grease and a little hard work!"
"And we'll be eatin' in a while."

"You're my little helper!"
"So I'll let you stir the sauce."
"Just remember what I tell you."
"Cause Mama is the boss!"

Mama's Meatball Recipe

Ingredients for the Meatballs

	Traditional Meat Recipe	🍃 Plant-Based Vegan Recipe
a.	2 lbs. ground meat (meatloaf mix consisting of beef, pork and veal is recommended)	2 12-oz. packages of plant-based meat such as Beyond Beef or Impossible Beef. *You can also use eggplant as a meat substitution, see Eggplant Preparation below* *🍆
b.	3 eggs	4.5 oz. Just Egg Plant-Based Scramble Liquid 🍃
c.	1 cup breadcrumbs (Italian seasoned breadcrumbs is recommended)	1 cup dairy-free vegan breadcrumbs (Italian seasoned if available) 🍃
d.	2 tablespoons fresh chopped parsley	2 tablespoons fresh chopped parsley
e.	1 tablespoon fresh chopped basil	1 tablespoon fresh chopped basil
f.	1 teaspoon garlic powder	1 teaspoon garlic powder
g.	½ cup grated Parmesan/Romano cheese	¼ cup nutritional yeast 🍃
h.	¼ teaspoon salt	¼ teaspoon salt
i.	¼ teaspoon pepper	¼ teaspoon pepper
j.	½ cup (or so) non-fat milk	½ cup (or so) nut milk or water 🍃
k.	¼ cup (or so) olive oil (for frying only)	¼ cup (or so) olive oil (for frying only)

🍃*Eggplant Preparation🍆

1. Wash and peel 2 medium to large eggplants; dice in small cubes. Then do one of following:
   - For firmer meatballs, add the eggplant to a nonstick pan with 1 tbsp. olive oil, and a dash each of salt, pepper and garlic powder; sauté for 4-6 minutes; put in food processor for a 5-10 seconds to blend; let cool; use in place of ground meat.
   - For softer meatballs, parboil the diced eggplant for 2-3 minutes (do not overcook), drain and press to remove liquid; mash or put in food processor for 5-10 seconds to puree; let cool. Reduce liquid items in b. and j. above to a few tbsp. otherwise, the mix may be too mushy.
2. Use the eggplant mixture along with all the other ingredients b. through j. above in place of ground meat for your meatballs. If eggplant is too soft, add some breadcrumbs.

For the Tomato Sauce or "Gravy", you will need:

1 or 2 28-oz. cans crushed tomatoes
   (Suggestion: Tuttoroso brand)
3 or 4 28-oz cans plain tomato sauce
   (For thinner sauce, use 4 cans tomato sauce and 1 can crushed tomatoes; for thicker sauce, use 3 cans tomato sauce and 2 cans crushed tomatoes)
¼ cup chopped white onion
2-3 tablespoons olive oil
2 tablespoons fresh chopped parsley
2 tablespoons fresh chopped basil
2 gloves of fresh garlic, chopped
2-3 whole basil leaves
Optional: Pinch of sugar

Other Suggested Dinner Supplies to Have On Hand:

1 lb. box of your favorite pasta
   (Suggestions: angel hair, spaghetti, linguini angel hair or other fun shapes such as penne, rigatoni, cavatappi, farfalle or fusilli)
Loaf of fresh Italian bread, sliced

Step 1: Prepare the Sauce ("Gravy")

- ❖ In an extra-large 8 to 10-quart pot), add 2-3 tablespoons olive oil and ¼ cup chopped white onion; simmer for 3-5 minutes on medium heat.
- ❖ Add the 5 cans of tomato sauce and crushed tomatoes, and gently mix with a large wooden spoon.
- ❖ Add the remaining ingredients (parsley, basil, garlic, whole basil leaves, and the optional pinch of sugar). Stir and cover with a lid. Simmer on medium to low heat, stirring occasionally.

Step 2: Make the Meatballs

- ❖ In an extra-large bowl, add the first meatball ingredient a. (ground meat, plant-based meat, or eggplant mixture).
- ❖ Then add ingredient b. (eggs/egg substitute) and all other dry ingredients c. to i. (breadcrumbs, parsley, basil, garlic powder, grated cheese/nutritional yeast, salt and pepper). Do not add the liquid ingredient j. just yet.
- ❖ With freshly washed hands, mix the meatball meat and other ingredients together. Add the milk (or nut milk/water) slowly, as needed, until the mix is not too hard and not too soft.
- ❖ One by one, grab a scoop of meatball mix and roll it into a ball in your hands. Place the rolled meatballs on a large flat dish or pan.
- ❖ Remember to wash hands frequently especially when touching dishes and utensils.

Mama's Meatball Recipe, continued

Step 3: Fry the Meatballs

- ❖ In a large frying pan, heat the olive oil or low to medium heat.
- ❖ Using a large spoon or freshly washed hands, carefully transfer a few meatballs at a time to the pan with oil.
- ❖ Brown the meatballs, carefully turning them with a spoon.

  Note: As an alternative to frying the meatballs, you can also brown the meatballs in the oven on a non-stick pan for 20-30 minutes on 350°.

Step 4: Add the Meatballs to the Sauce

- ❖ Once the meatballs are a light brown color, carefully transfer the meatballs to the large pot with the sauce. You can transfer a few meatballs at a time as they are cooked.
- ❖ Simmer the meatballs in the sauce for approximately 30-45 minutes, on medium to low heat, stirring occasionally.

Step 5: Prepare the Pasta

- ❖ Fill a large pot with water and bring to a boil.
- ❖ Add the pasta shape of your choice and cook until al dente.
- ❖ Drain the pasta and toss with some sauce and meatballs. **Enjoy!**

Many Thanks!

I hope you have enjoyed reading this book, and if you followed the recipe, I hope you and your family enjoyed the pasta and meatballs!

Can I ask for a small favor? Could you please consider leaving a review, or providing some brief feedback on what you liked about the book? I understand that you may have purchased this book online or in a bookstore, so there are several ways that you can help.

If you purchased the book online, you can leave a review on the website where you purchased the book. Online reviews help online rankings, which customers look for when they decide to make a purchase. If you purchased the book in a bookstore, consider letting the bookstore know how much you enjoyed the book. Reviews and feedback are so important and will truly help me provide more books like this one!

You can also contact me here: geni.us/askamelia and let me know how you and your family liked the book. I welcome your feedback and any questions you may have.

You can also find me on Instagram by searching for @ameliagwrites or go to: www.instagram.com/ameliagwrites

Thank you!

Other Books in the

Bella and Mia Adventure Series!

Silly Willy Apple Cake

Mia and her daughter Bella go apple picking at a farm. Bella loves to be silly. She laughs as she balances an apple on her arm, and asks 'What can we make? What can we make?" Mama says "an apple cake"! So, home they go, to mix and bake, and soon they are eating apple cake! *Apple Cake Recipe Included!*

❄ Snowflakes With Sugar ❄

Mia and Bella are decorating for the holidays and decide to make a special treat which is a family tradition. Mix flour, eggs, vanilla, sugar, a little of this and a little that, plus lots of love, and what do you get? Can you guess what it is? What happens when the doorbell rings? *Recipe included for this surprise treat!*

* * * * *

You can find all books in this series here: geni.us/bellamiaseries

Follow me here: geni.us/authoramelia

Questions? Contact me here: geni.us/askamelia

Made in the USA
Middletown, DE
16 November 2024